Jewish
Baby Book

Jewish Symbols and Holidays

Learn (to read and speak) everyday
Hebrew words!

ENGLISH and HEBREW
For English speakers

Everyday Hebrew Books

Donut

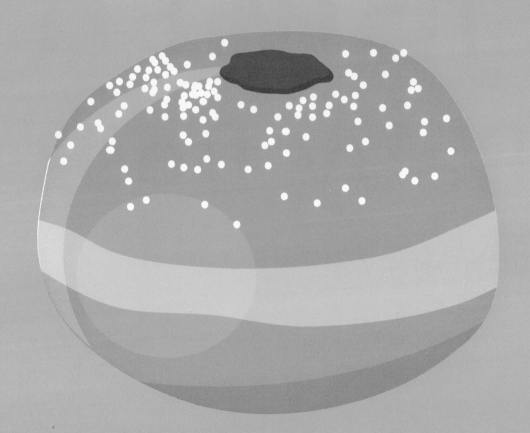

סֻפְגָּנִיָּיה
suf-gan-ee-iah

Dreidel

seh-vivon סְבִיבוֹן

The Oil jug

כַּד הַשֶּׁמֶן
Kad - Ha-sh-men

Channukah money

seh-vivon דְּמֵי חֲנֻכָּה

latke

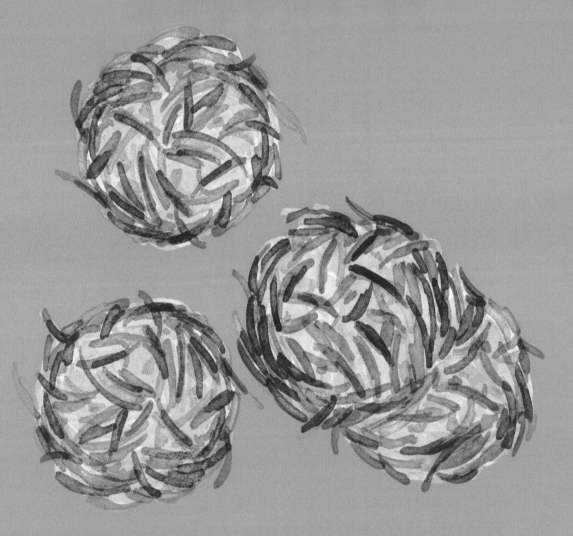

leh-viva לְבִיבָה

Chanukah lamp

Ha-nuk-ee-iah חֲנֻכִּיָּה

sukkah

sukkah סֻכָּה

The four varieties

אַרְבַּעַת-הַמִּינִים

Arr-bat - Ha-minim

Scroll

Megillah מְגִלָּה

Hamantasch

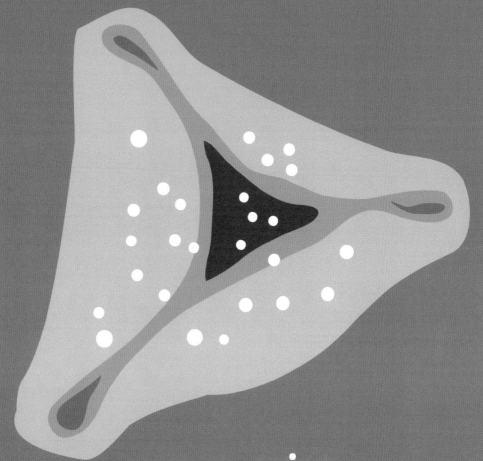

אֹזֶן הָמָן

Ozen - Haman

Grager

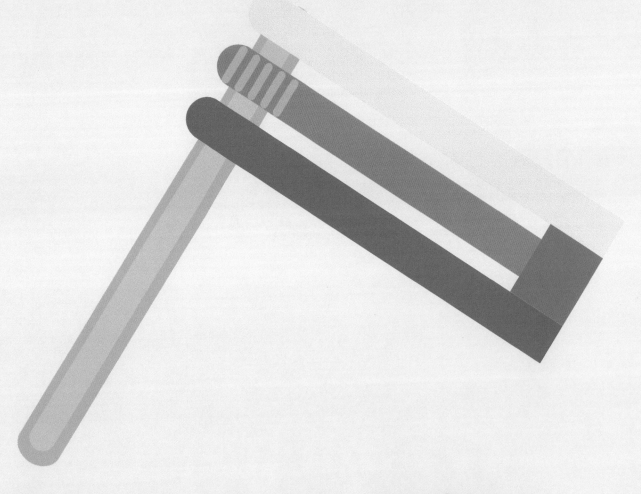

Ra-a-shan רַעֲשָׁן

mask

Masckha מַסֵכָה

mishloach manot

מִשְׁלוֹחַ מָנוֹת

Passover Seder plate

צַלַחַת פֶּסַח
Tsalahat - Passackh

Matza

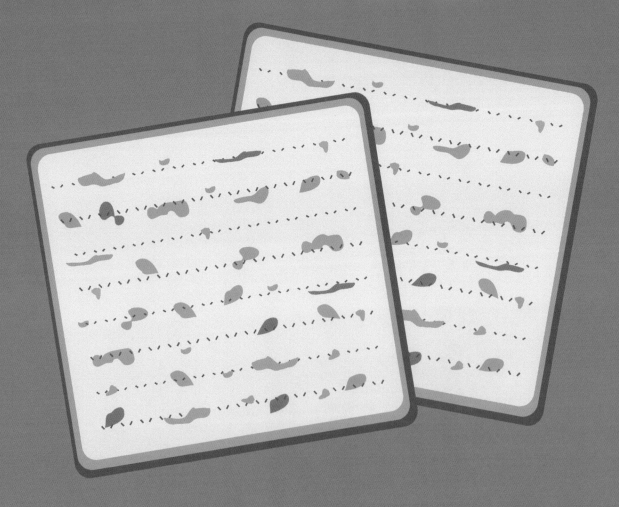

Matza מַצָּה

Passover Haggada

Haggada הַגָּדָה

Elijah's Cup

גְּבִיעַ-אֵלִיָּהוּ

Ga-vi-ya - Eliyahu

Tablets of Stone

לוּחוֹת הַבְּרִית
Lu-ckhot - Ha-brit

Honey

Dvash דְּבַשׁ

Pomegranate

Rimon רִימוֹן

Wine

Ya-inn ワイン

Synagogue

בֵּית כְּנֶסֶת

Beit - knesset

Shofar

Shofar שׁוֹפָר

Israeli flag

דֶּגֶל יִשְׂרָאֵל
Degel - Israel

Mezuzah

Mezuzah מְזוּזָה

Apple

Tapu-ackh תַּפּוּחַ

Star of David

מָגֵן דָּוִד
Magen - David

Challah

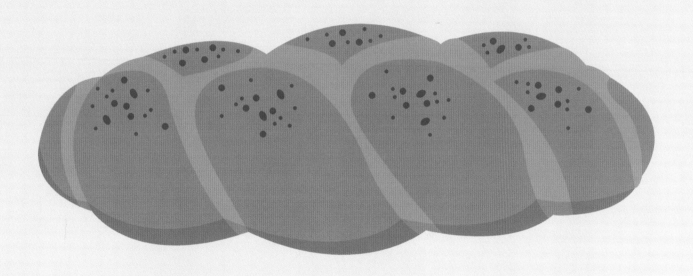

חַלָּה
Challah

Yarmulke

Kippa קִיפָּה

Prayer shawl

Talit טַלִּית

Printed in Great Britain
by Amazon

41948689R00021